USING AN AUTO-INJECTOR

BY HARRIET BRUNDLE

HUMAN BODY HELPERS

BookLife
PUBLISHING

©2019
BookLife Publishing Ltd.
King's Lynn
Norfolk PE30 4LS

All rights reserved.
Printed in Malaysia.

A catalogue record for this book is available from the British Library.

ISBN: 978-1-78637-712-8

Written by:
Harriet Brundle

Edited by:
John Wood

Designed by:
Danielle Rippengill

All facts, statistics, web addresses and URLs in this book were verified as valid and accurate at time of writing. No responsibility for any changes to external websites or references can be accepted by either the author or publisher.

The author of this book is not a medically trained professional. If you have any questions about auto-injectors, please see your doctor.

IMAGE CREDITS

All images are courtesy of Shutterstock.com, unless otherwise specified. With thanks to Getty Images, Thinkstock Photo and iStockphoto.
Front Cover & 1 – Beatriz Gascon J, NikaMooni, Makyzz, LOVE YOU. Wilma – Makyzz. Ahmed – LOVE YOU. 2 – Makyzz. 5 – Zhe Vasylieva. 6 – Satenik Guzhanina. 9 – Makyzz. 10 – EstherQueen999, Zhe Vasylieva. 14 – Iconic Bestiary. 15 – jehsomwang. 19 – Sudowoodo, Dicraftsman. 20 – robuart. 21 – Iconic Bestiary, Zhe Vasylieva. 22 – Zhe Vasylieva.

CONTENTS

PAGE 4 What Is an Allergy?

PAGE 6 What Is Anaphylaxis?

PAGE 8 What Is an Auto-Injector?

PAGE 10 How Do I Know I Need an Auto-Injector?

PAGE 12 How Does an Auto-Injector Work?

PAGE 14 How Do I Use My Auto-Injector?

PAGE 18 At the Hospital

PAGE 20 Dos and Don'ts

PAGE 22 Life After Your Allergy

PAGE 24 Glossary and Index

*Words that look like **this** can be found in the glossary on page 24.*

WHAT IS AN ALLERGY?

When you have an allergy, your body reacts to something that is usually harmless.

Your body thinks it needs to fight off what is causing the allergy. As a result, you feel the **symptoms** of having an allergy.

> Hi, I'm Wilma Windpipe. I connect your mouth and nose to your lungs.

For some people, eating certain foods can cause them to have an allergic reaction.

NUTS

If you are having a mild allergic reaction, you might sneeze, cough, have a rash or have itchy eyes. Lots of different things can cause an allergic reaction, including an insect sting, animal hair or grass.

WHAT IS ANAPHYLAXIS?

Anaphylaxis happens when you have a very bad allergic reaction.

Anaphylaxis symptoms can include: **wheezing,** stomach pain, feeling confused, getting a rash and feeling faint.

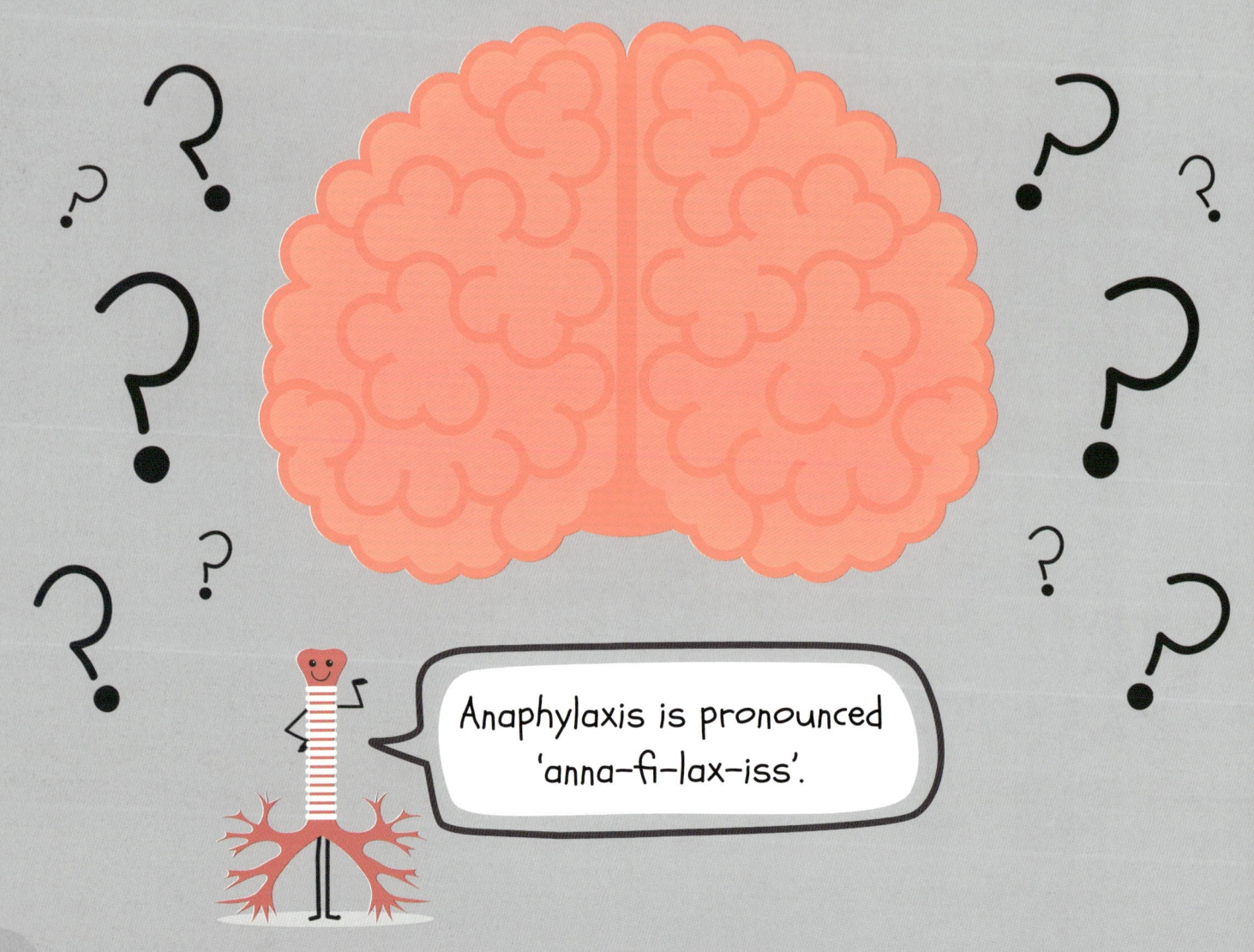

Anaphylaxis is pronounced 'anna-fi-lax-iss'.

Your lips, throat and tongue might **swell** too. This makes it difficult for you to breathe.

Anaphylaxis may come on suddenly and you can start feeling extremely poorly very quickly. If you feel any of the symptoms, it's important that you stay calm and get an adult straight away.

WHAT IS AN AUTO-INJECTOR?

Hi! I'm Ahmed and I'm a type of auto-injector! I'm used to help somebody during anaphylaxis.

Anyone can use an auto-injector to give an **injection**. An auto-injector injects the right amount of a medicine into your body, which helps you to feel better.

You should always carry your auto-injector with you and make sure that somebody with you knows how to use it. There is more than one type of auto-injector, so it's important that you and others with you know how to use yours properly.

If you're feeling the signs of anaphylaxis, it is also known as having an anaphylactic reaction.

HOW DO I KNOW I NEED AN AUTO-INJECTOR?

If you think you could be allergic to something, you will need to go to see a doctor. The doctor might carry out some tests to find out exactly what is causing your allergy.

You might be allergic to a particular type of food.

DOCTOR

The doctor might try different drops on your skin to see how your body reacts or ask you to change what you eat for a few weeks. If you need it, you'll be **prescribed** an auto-injector.

HOW DOES AN AUTO-INJECTOR WORK?

Ahmed, I need your help!

During an anaphylactic reaction, there is swelling around your airways. It causes the airways to get narrower. This makes it difficult for you to breathe.

Inside your auto-injector is a special type of medicine. When you inject it into your body, it quickly lessens the swelling around your airways, helping you to breathe more easily.

"Stay calm, Wilma. You'll be feeling better soon."

HOW DO I USE MY AUTO-INJECTOR?

Make sure you hold your auto-injector with your **dominant** hand. Take off the safety cap, and hold the auto-injector on the area you need to inject. This is usually your thigh.

Auto-injectors can usually be used through clothes.

SAFETY CAP

Push the auto-injector into your skin and hold it there until the medicine has gone into your body. After you have used your auto-injector, you should go to the hospital straight away.

"Don't worry, Wilma. I'll be right here!"

You may be able to use a second auto-injector if the first **dose** of medicine has not worked well enough. You usually need to wait several minutes before you use a second auto-injector.

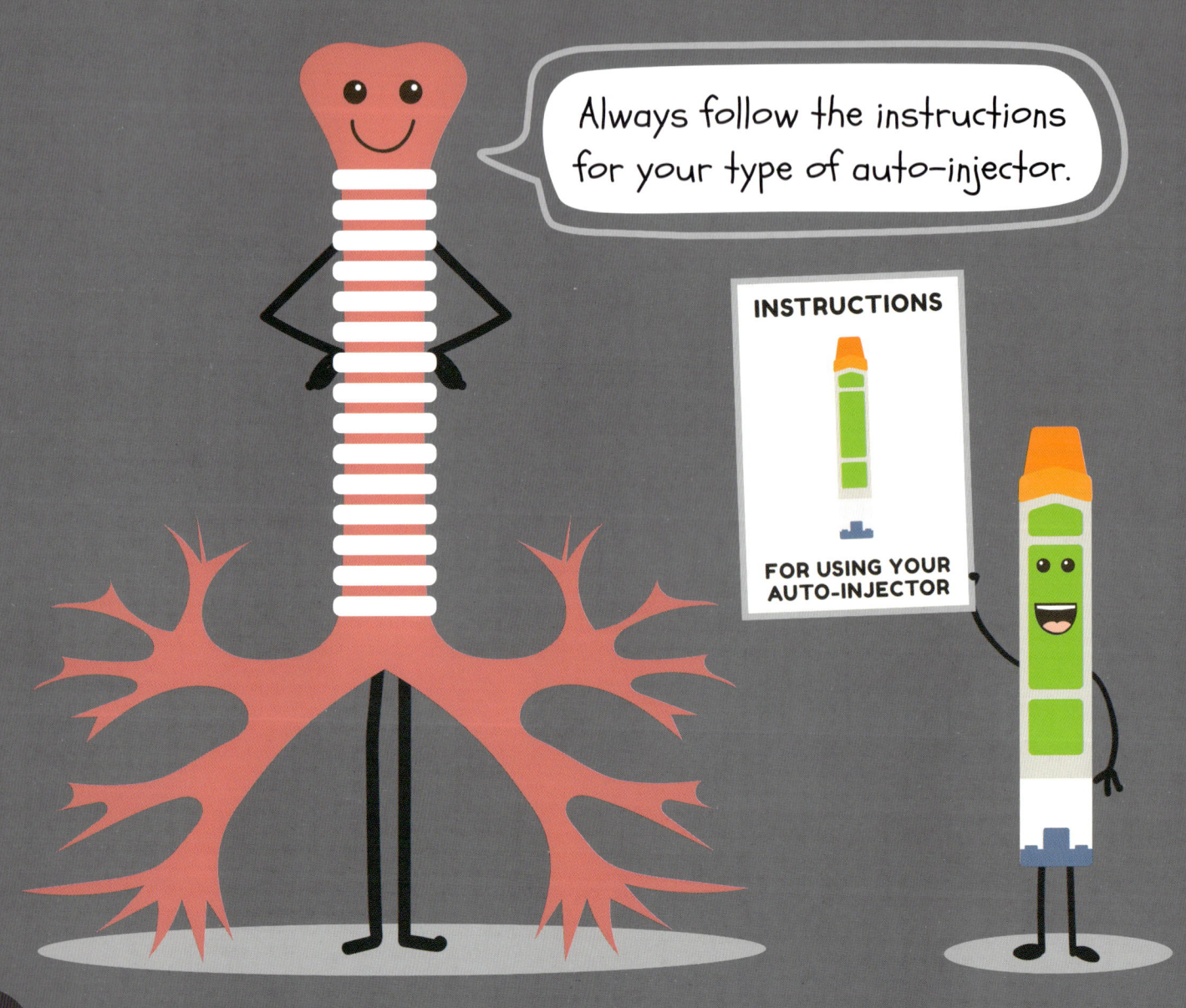

Always follow the instructions for your type of auto-injector.

INSTRUCTIONS FOR USING YOUR AUTO-INJECTOR

"You'll need to get another one of me straight away!"

The same auto-injector cannot be used more than once. After you have used yours, it's important that you take it to the hospital with you, where it can be **disposed of** safely.

AT THE HOSPITAL

"The doctors will take good care of you, Wilma."

When you get to the hospital, you may need to stay there for a few hours so the doctor can make sure your symptoms won't come back.

You might need to wear an **oxygen** mask for a while to help you breathe more easily. You may also need to have a blood test or some more medicine.

Thank you, Ahmed. I'm feeling much better already.

DOS AND DON'TS

DO play it safe! If you think you might be feeling the symptoms of anaphylaxis, tell an adult straight away as you may need to use your auto-injector.

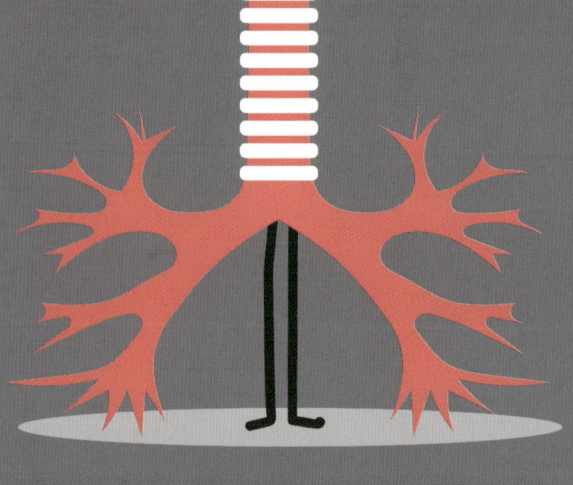

DON'T forget to carry your auto-injector with you at all times. If you have two auto-injectors, make sure you carry them both.

DO try to avoid anything you know could cause you to have an anaphylactic reaction. If you are allergic to a particular type of food, be extra careful when you're eating outside your home.

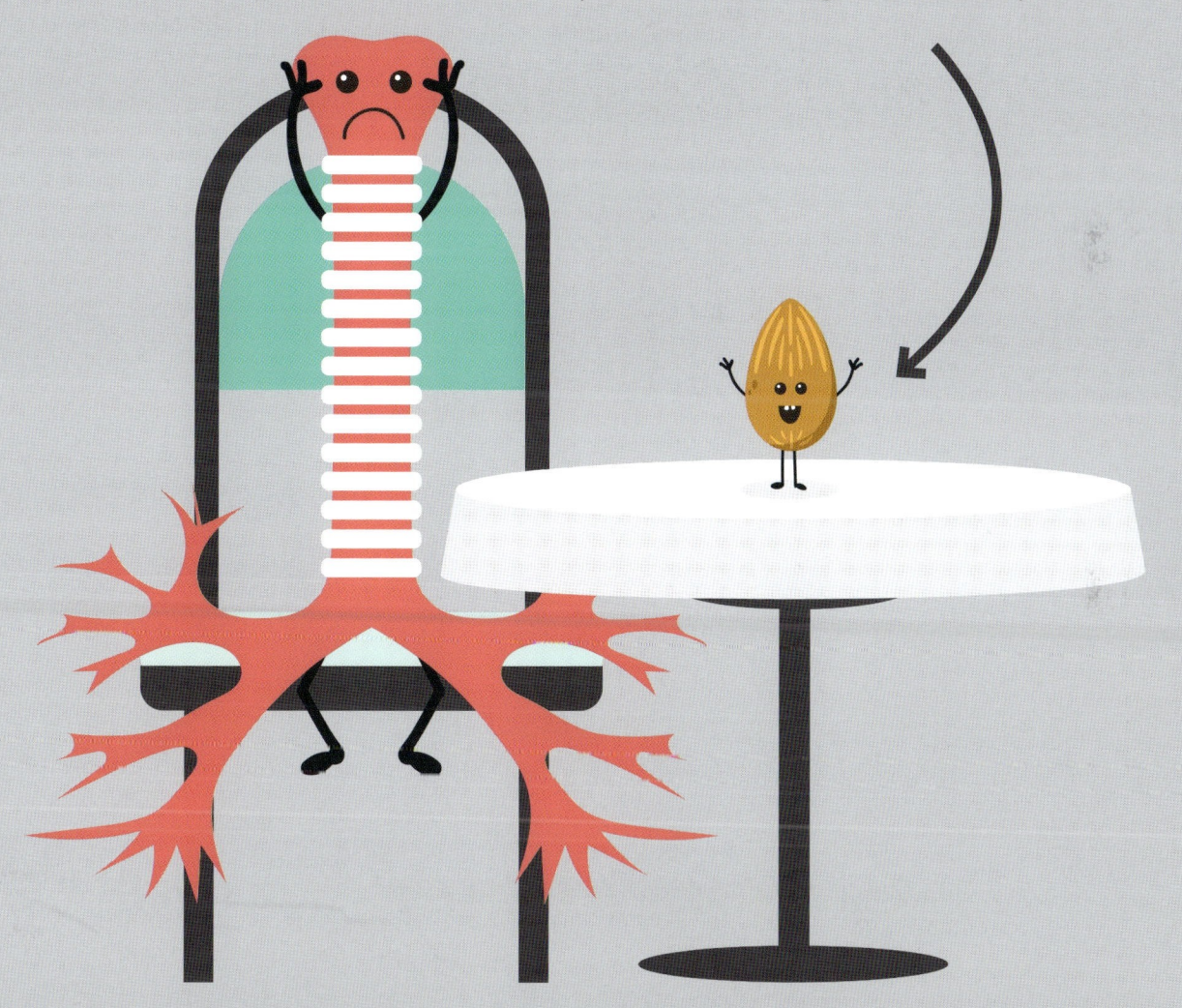

DON'T forget that you will need to get a new auto-injector after you have used yours.

LIFE AFTER YOUR ALLERGY

Some children can grow out of their allergies as they get older. This means that they no longer feel the same symptoms when they come into contact with the cause of their allergy.

"Thanks for your help, Ahmed."

"You're welcome, Wilma!"

Some people have an allergy for all their lives. Most allergies can be kept under control by taking steps to avoid any **triggers** and using the right medicine.

GLOSSARY

DISPOSED OF	thrown away
DOMINANT	more powerful
DOSE	an amount of medicine
INJECTION	the act of putting something into your body, such as medicine, using a needle
OXYGEN	a gas you need to breathe to stay alive
PRESCRIBED	given instructions for medicine to be given to somebody
SWELL	get bigger
SYMPTOMS	the signs of an illness
TRIGGERS	things that cause something else to happen
WHEEZING	breathing with a whistling or gasping sound

INDEX

AIRWAYS 12–13
DOCTORS 10–11, 18
FOOD 5, 10, 21
HOSPITALS 15, 17, 18
LIPS 7
MEDICINE 8, 13, 15–16, 19, 23
NUTS 5
RASH 5–6
TESTS 10, 19
THROAT 7
TONGUE 7